30 Poems by Christian Morgenstern

Translated & Illustrated by Betsy Hulick

SHIRES PRESS
4869 Main Street
P.O. Box 2200
Manchester Center, VT 05255
www.northshire.com

30 Poems by Christian Morgenstern

ISBN Number: 978-0-9860662-0-7

Printed in the United States of America

A Short Introduction

The poems in this book are about animals and things, and two gentlemen, Korf and Palmer. The animals and things are familiar to everyone, but they are imagined in unfamiliar ways. Palmer and Korf will be new acquaintances, but the qualities of pure feeling in the first and pure thought in the second are to be found in mixed degree in everyone; and were evenly balanced in Christian Morgenstern, from whose work this sampling is drawn, in the hope that a native German talent may agreeably visit in English-speaking lands.

Table of Contents

for Morgenstern fans everywhere
but especially Rhino Küffner.

The Aesthetic Anaconda

An anaconda
sent a Honda
to Jane Fonda
(the motorcycle, not the car)

not because
the creature was
unhinged by passion for the star
(although it happens all the time) -

The case was worse.
Mad for verse,
he couldn't resist the triple rhyme.

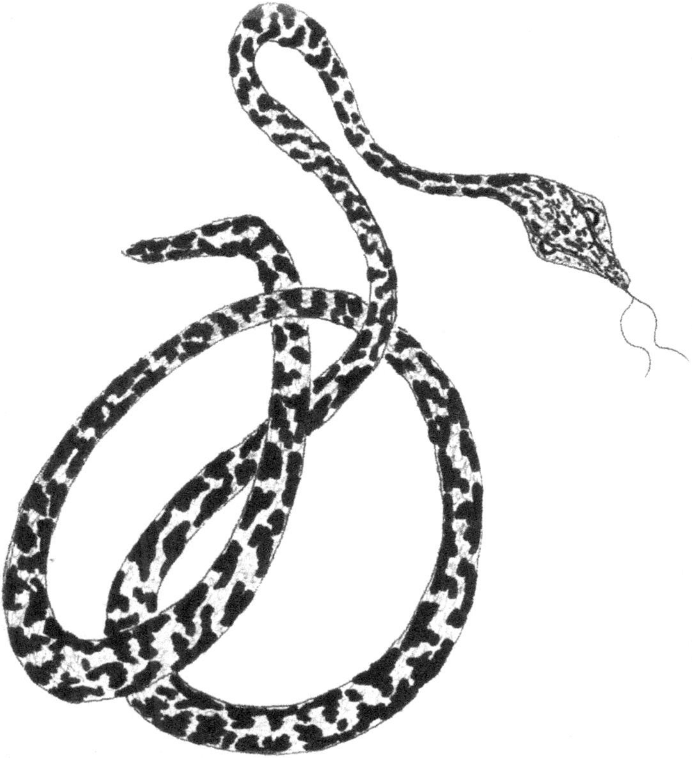

Water

Water's character is odd:
It utters not a single word.
But if it did, without a doubt,
every pipe and water spout

would gurgle love love love alone
and that's not news to anyone;
which goes to show, lest we forget,
water's way is not all wet.

The Rocking Chair on the Deserted Terrace

I am a rocking chair, rocking alone,
I rock in the wind,
in the wind.

I rock on the terrace, my wood slapping stone,
and I rock in the wind,
in the wind.

All the day long, I rock and I rock,
and the boughs of the linden trees crackle and knock,
I wonder what else in the world likes to rock
in the wind,
in the wind
in the wind.

The Sigh

A Sigh went out to skate one night.
His hopes were high, his heart was light.
Round and round the pond he went,
carefree, calm and confident.

All at once he stopped. A name
kindled in his heart a flame.
The ice began to crack and melt.
He sank and drowned with all he felt.

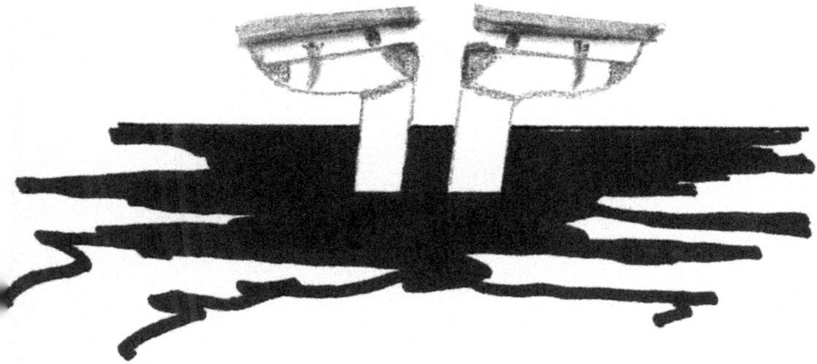

The Planet of Flies

Daily life on the Planet of Flies
is surely very curious:
The way that we treat flies on ours,
there, the flies treat us.

There, amassed in sticky clumps,
we cling to dangling strips of paper
and hover over garbage dumps,
ODing on the vapor.

Even so, our lot fares better
among their kind than theirs does here:
We don't get baked in cookie batter
or chugalugged with beer.

Fate

The thunder, tongued with fire, spoke:
"I bring the light to barnyard folk."

A bullock standing in his stall
was scorched to blackness, horns and all.

Now he broods incessantly:
Who did this thing? And why to me?

Soliloquy of a Snail

Shall I go out?
Shall I stay in?
Day out today?
Day in today?
Stay in today?
Go out today?
Say I stay in
will I miss out?
Suppose I go out
will I want in?
Stay in go out
dayindayoutstayingoout .....

(The snail becomes so hopelessley confused by his own thoughts that he is unable to reach a decision and postpones the question indefinitely.)

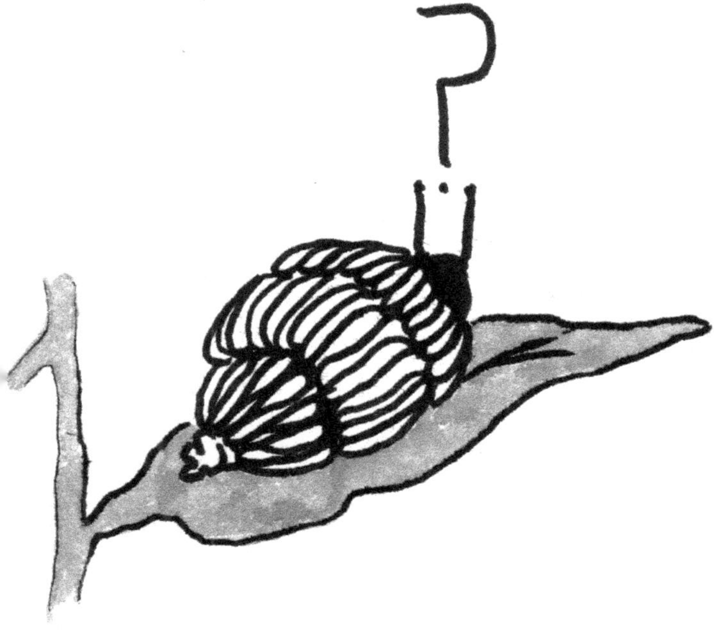

The Sparrow and the Kangaroo

In the zoo, a kangaroo
sits looking at a sparrow, who,

for his part, perched atop a fence,
finds the focus too intense

and ducks his head, uncertain why
his presence should attract this eye:

The sparrow gives himself a shake.
The heat is on, make no mistake.

Perhaps, he thinks, the kangaroo
is contemplating sparrow stew?

Not thirty minutes later, though,
for reasons too obscure to know,

the kangaroo has turned his head
to look at something else instead.

Palmer

Palmer pauses by a brook,
and shakes out his red handkerchief.
It shows a reader with his book
beneath a drifting autumn leaf.

Palmer dares not blow his nose.
He numbers in the ranks of those
who, caught off guard by beauty's presence,
deliver up their souls to reverence.

He folds the handkerchief in four
and pockets it, still virgin stuff
And what hard heart would fault him for
an unblown nose as he walks off?

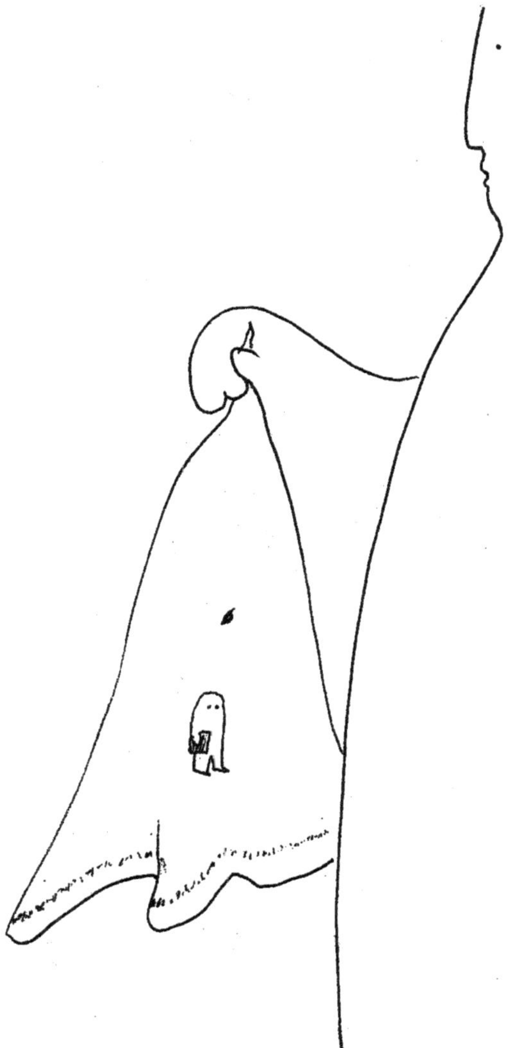

Weatherwise I

A tourist in New York's financial district,
Palmer thinks: Good grief, it's raining torrents!
and opens his umbrella for protection.

But not a leaf is stirred by windy currents
and clouds are visible in no direction.
Even so, the situation warrants

cautious measures: In an atmosphere
awash with throngs of wily financiers,
getting soaked is not a groundless fear.

Weatherwise II

Palmer has a liking for bad weather;
It makes the world more peaceful altogether.
Strain and stress substantially subside,
and human posture is more dignified.

The mini-heaven of a man's umbrella
symbolically affects his inner core;
the all-embracing one, however stellar,
is far too distant for a close rapport.

Therefore Palmer, when it's raining hard,
perambulates the boulevard,
rejoicing in the picture of mankind
so much more cosmo-logically aligned.

Palma Kunkel

Palma is a relative
of Palmer's on the Kunkel side -
however, she prefers to live
alone and unidentified.

The pages of the chronicler
omit her therefore: Only when
she leaves the shadows, as it were,
can she be said to come in ken.

But there has been no trace of her
to date, nor will there be in future;
so very private is her nature,
in even naming her, we err.

Fauna Costumes

Among the pastimes Palmer cherishes
(furnishing two tailors with their custom)
is dressing up in fauna costumes.

From time to time, suited as a raven,
he'll settle on an oak tree's topmost branch
and cast an eye across the starry heavens.

At other times, he'll rest his shaggy head
on broad, intrepid paws, a St. Bernard
lost in dreams of snowy Alpine rescue;

or in his own backyard, he'll spin a web
from silky threads, and nestling in its midst,
peer out, a mild reclusive spider.

Then too, he'll circumnavigate his pond,
a carp, with flat, exaggerated eyes,
fed by children, tossing him their breadcrumbs.

And then again, appareled as a stork,
he'll fit himself beneath an airship's prow,
and slowly, slowly, travel so to Egypt.

Foreign Countries

Palmer visits, somewhere in the north,
a foreign country with his neighbor Korf.

So unfamiliar is the idiom
he can't make out a word that's said to him.

Nor - alas! - can Korf (who only went
to eke the rhyme out) tell him what is meant.

But just this circumstance is what delights
Palmer most. Back home again, he writes

his journal up: "Heart, as always, full.
Fresh evidence: Life is wonderful!"

Korf's Clock

Korf invents a superclock.
Double hands adorn its dial.
With one set, time advances while
the other ticks its backward tock.

At two o'clock, it's therefore ten.
at three, it's nine o'clock as well.
One glance suffices to dispel
the terrors time inspires in men,

for Korf's clock's Janus-like precision
(the rationale of its design)
is tuned so very very fine
time self-destructs from indecision.

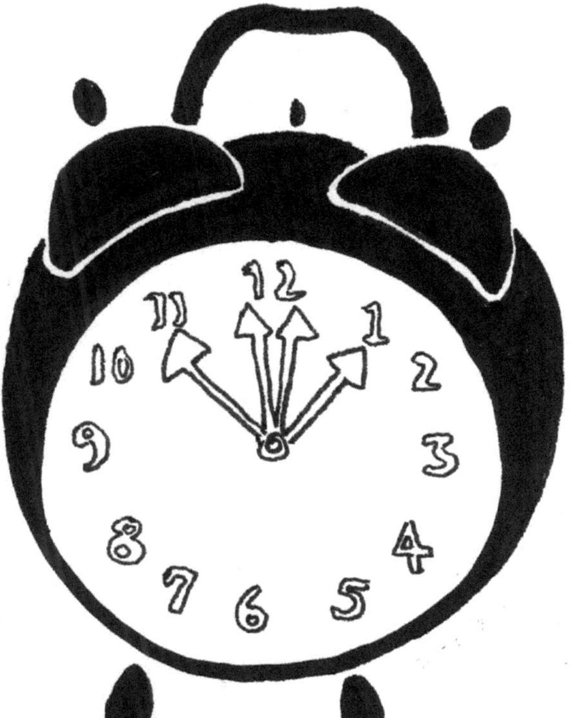
12
1
2
3
4
5
6
7
8
9
10
11

Palmer's Clock

Palmer's clock is different, viz,
as tender as mimosa is,

it cannot tolerate distress
but always answers Help! with Yes;

has, too, been known (when prayers are said)
to lag behind or leap ahead

one hour, two hours - even three -
so keen it is in empathy.

A clock it is in every point
but one: It cannot disappoint.

A thing of cogs and gears and wheels,
it has a ticking heart that feels.

The Mousetrap

I

A mouse has been at Palmer's cheese:
the Emmentalers and the Bries.

His neighbor Korf, at pains to end
the lamentations of his friend,

supplies him with a violin
and concert-cage to play it in.

Beneath the vault of heaven, hark!
Palmer fiddles in the dark.

His inspiration soars, and lo!
the mouse creeps in to hear him bow.

Behind her back, a grating drops
soundlessly. The music stops.

Palmer dozes in his chair.
Silence settles on the pair.

The Mousetrap

II

Korf arrives with morning light,
removes the structure from its site

and packs it in a horse-drawn van
without disturbing mouse or man.

Transported by the sturdy horse,
they reach the forest in due course,

where Korf calls halt and sets them free
beside a brook, beneath a tree.

The mouse leaps out ahead of Palmer,
who follows after, somewhat calmer.

She shows no symptoms of distress
adapting to the wilderness,

and he goes home, a happy man,
with Korf, the driver, horse and van.

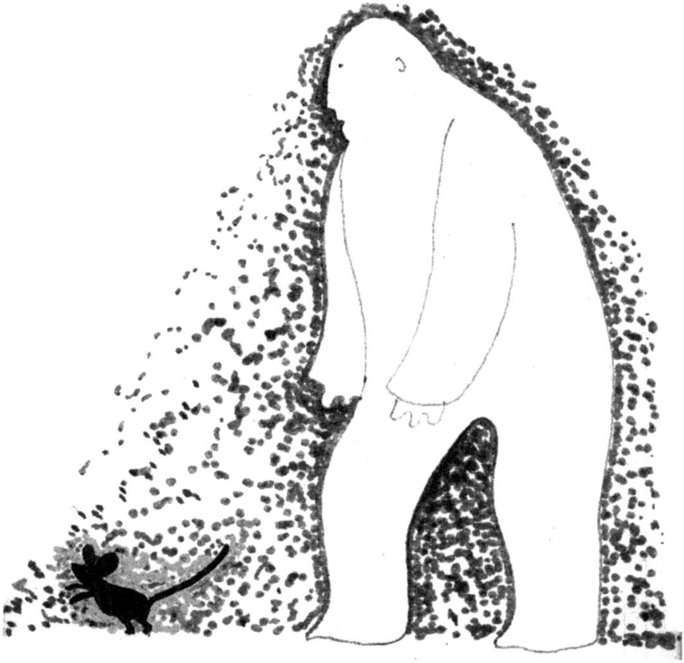

The Two Feasts

Korf and Palmer, hosting each a feast,
agree on theme, but disagree on venue:

Palmer's worldwide invitation list
makes no exclusions - still, it has a twist:
Instead of sitting to a rich repast,
the guests appoint a day on which to fast.
An anti-hunger fund completes the menu.

Korf, however, goes among the poor,
outcasts, beggars, casualties of war,
and pleads with them to give up one day's ration
of bitter rancor, throwing wide the door
that locks in every impulse to compassion.

Giving, not receiving, both hosts think,
furnishes the choicest food and drink,
and only feasts of this uncommon sort
can comfort and sustain the hungry heart.

Korf Collected

Korf, admiring erudition,
collects himself in an Edition
(the print of course is very fine).
Its covers close across his spine
and pages open to the side
like wings, voluminously wide.
Burdened by the literal weight
of learning when he stands up straight,
he finds, as soon as he reclines,
an easy read between the lines.

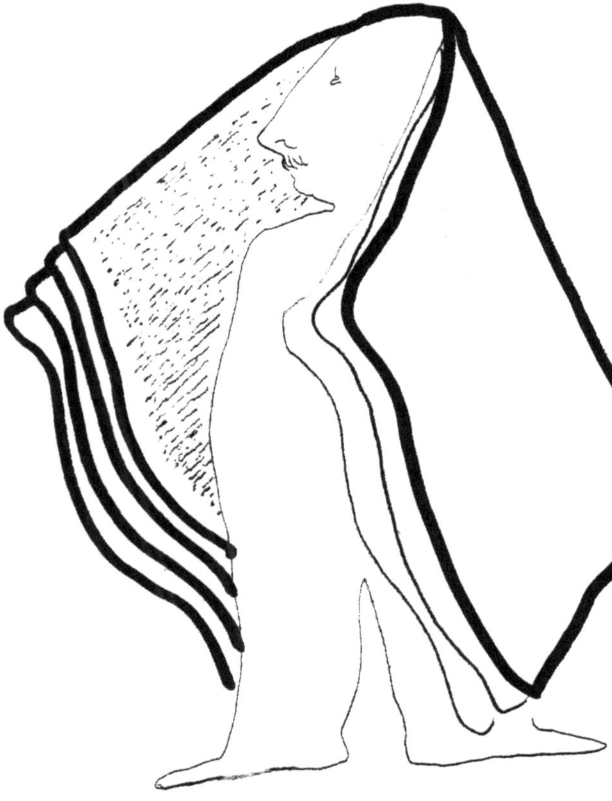

The Books of Western Man

The sight of books stacked side by side
compels von Korf to run and hide.

He can't abide the hundredweight
of volumes, cannot penetrate

the mystery posed by such dense rows
of hardened poetry and prose.

This crush of matter, tome on tome!
Can spirit find in it a home?

he wonders: Spirit's self is light,
and heavy-clad, cannot take flight,

but Western man, alas! alak!
must ever bind it front to back.

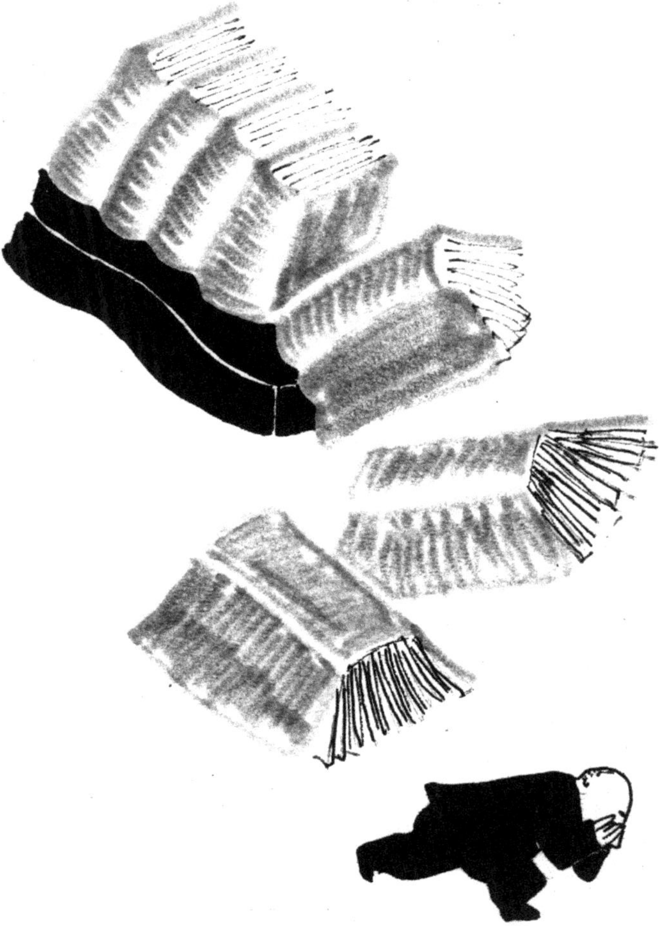

The Obedient Giant

Korf 's acquainted with a giant
whose wife hand-feeds him day and night
whatever she dislikes on sight.

This giant is so compliant
he opens wide while she inserts
behind his teeth hors d'oeuvres, desserts,

and entrees from the ready store
of things she has no liking for,
and there's not much she likes or wants,

from flying ants to elephants:
Mountains, highways, rivers, trees,
whole municipalities

with their inhabitants and houses
are lodged in her complacent spouse's
mouth, alongside beards and wigs,

cutlery and oil rigs.
In short, this husband's mouth of hers
accommodates a universe.

She dislikes Korf, and in he goes:
presto, open! presto, close!
down the hatch with all the rest -

But Korf is spirit, spirit's blessed,
and that's the single reason why
he reemerges by and by.

Windy Exchange

You haven't traveled round the globe?
Seen Nairobi? Crossed the Gobi?
Swept across Tibet's plateau?

I haven't, no – don't guess I will.
I'm just a local wind, you know.
Have you seen Charlie's Bar & Grill?

Can't say I have, child. Well, so long.
Lisbon - Amsterdam - Hong Kong...

The Two Roots

Within a wood
two pinetree roots
old and gnarled
are in cahoots.

What overhead
is said, beneath
the two repeat
on knobby breath.

A sqirrel who sits
on nearby rocks
knits the roots
a pair of socks.

The one goes crack,
the other, creak –
enough of talk
to last a week.

The Lion

A calendar upon the wall
displays a lion majestical.

On August seventh he surveys
the room with a commanding gaze,

effectively reminding us
his reign continues glorious.

The Picket Fence

Once, there was a picket fence
with missing space between each slat
for looking through at this and that
conveniencing pedestrians.

An architect who happened by
seized his opportunity,
and stole the missing elements
to build a house at no expense.

The pickets meantime left in place
without interpolated space
nakedly endured disgrace.
Public outcry in the case

was loud, divisive and intense.
With imperturbable sang froid,
the architect removed his talents
to Afri- or Ameri-ca.

The Two Donkeys

A donkey feeling melancholy
told his wife: "Let's face it, Molly,

You're an ass and so am I.
There's nothing for it. Let's go die."

But such a morbid fit soon passes:
They lived on happily as asses.

Wish for a Monument

When I am dead and gone, my dear,
make a sugarloaf of me
and set it in the wide, salt sea.

so in the depths, where it shall sink,
a hundred startled fishes think
it's sweet fresh water that they drink,

then caught in Hamburg or in Bremen
and gone to nourish men and women,
I'll come among my kind again.

Whereas, if I were made of granite,
I'd only serve as an excuse
for pigeons and dyspeptic critics
to rain on me their foul abuse.

The Hen

In a department store, never meant for her,
a hen goes back and forth.
Where O where is the manager:
Won't she incur
the shoppers' wrath?
Oh dear, Oh dear, don't say it's so.
Let's cry aloud: Our hearts go out to her.
A hen can't know when she's *de trop*!

The Sniffles

A pair of sniffles on a terrace
lay in wait like terrorists

to catch their man. As he appeared,
they leaped, alighting on his beard.

He sneezed in greeting. Ah-ah-
tchoo!
Now I ask you: Who caught who?

The Knee

A knee goes lonely through the world
an ordinary knee.
It's not a tent, it's not a tree,
it's just a plain old knee.

A man was once shot up in war;
of all his parts, the knee alone
remained intact, as if it were
a holy saint's or martyr's bone.

Since then this knee has traveled far
this ordinary knee.
It's not a tent, it's not a tree,
it's just a knee, and there you are.

Appendix

1. Das aesthetische Wiesel

Ein Wiesel
saß auf einem Kiesel
inmitten Bachgeriesel.

Wißt ihr,
weshalb?

Das Mondkalb
verriet es mir
im stillen:

Das raffinier-
te Tier
tats um des Reimes willen.

2. Das Wasser

Ohne Wort, ohne Wort
rinnt das Wasser immerfort;
andernfalls, andernfalls
sprach es doch nichts andres als:

Bier und Brot, Lieb und Treu, –
und das wäre auch nicht neu.
Dieses zeigt, dieses zeigt,
daß das Wasser besser schweigt.

3. Der Schaukelstuhl auf der verlassenen Terrasse

Ich bin ein einsamer Schaukelstuhl
und wackel im Winde,
im Winde.

Auf der Terrasse, da ist es kuhl,
und ich wackel im Winde,
im Winde.

Und ich wackel und nackel den ganzen Tag.
Und es nackelt und rackelt die Linde.
Wer weiß, was sonst wohl noch wackeln mag
im Winde,
im Winde,
im Winde.

4. Der Seufzer

Ein Seufzer lief Schlittschuh auf nächtlichem Eis
und träumte von Liebe und Freude.
Es war an dem Stadtwall, und schneeweiß
glänzten die Stadtwallgebäude.

Der Seufzer dacht' an ein Maidelein
und blieb erglühend stehen.
Da schmolz die Eisbahn unter ihm ein –
und er sank – und ward nimmer gesehen.

5. Auf dem Fliegenplaneten

Auf dem Fliegenplaneten,
da geht es dem Menschen nicht gut:
Denn was er hier der Fliege,
die Fliege dort ihm tut.

An Bändern voll Honig kleben
die Menschen dort allesamt,
und andre sind zum Verleben
in süßliches Bier verdammt.

In Einem nur scheinen die Fliegen
dem Menschen vorauszustehn:
Man bäckt uns nicht in Semmeln,
noch trinkt man uns aus Versehn.

6. Schicksal

Der Wolke Zickzackzunge spricht:
“Ich bringe dir, mein Hammel, Licht.”

Der Hammel, der im Stalle stand,
ward links und hinten schwarz gebrannt.

Sein Leben grübelt er seitdem:
warum ihm dies geschah von wem?

7. Gespräch einer Hausschnecke mit sich selbst

Soll i aus meim Hause raus?
Soll i aus meim Hause nit raus?
Einen Schritt raus?
Lieber nit raus?
Hausenitraus –
Hauseraus
Hauseritraus
Hausenaus
Rauserauserauserause ...

(Die Schnecke verfängt sich in ihren eigenen Gedanken oder vielmehr diese gehen mit ihr dermaßen durch, daß sie die weitere Entscheidung der Frage verschieben muß.)

8. Der Sperling und das Känguruh

In seinem Zaun das Känguruh
es hockt und guckt dem Sperling zu.

Der Sperling sitzt auf dem Gebäude –
doch ohne sonderliche Freude.

Vielmehr, er fühlt, den Kopf geduckt,
wie ihn das Känguruh beguckt.

Der Sperling sträubt den Federflaus –
die Sache ist auch gar zu kraus.

Ihm ist, als ob er kaum noch säße ...
Wenn nun das Känguruh ihn fräße?!

Doch dieses dreht nach einer Stunde
den Kopf aus irgend einem Grunde,

vielleicht auch ohne tiefern Sinn,
nach einer andern Richtung hin.

9. Palmström

Palmström steht an einem Teiche
und entfaltet groß ein rotes Taschentuch:
Auf dem Tuch ist eine Eiche
dargestellt sowie ein Mensch mit einem Buch.

Palmström wagt nicht, sich hineinzuschneuzen.
Er gehört zu jenen Käuzen,
die oft unvermittelt-nackt
Ehrfurcht vor dem Schönen packt.

Zärtlich faltet er zusammen,
was er eben erst entbreitet.
Und kein Fühlender wird ihn verdammen,
weil er ungeschneuzt entschreitet.

10. Bona fide

Palmström geht durch eine fremde Stadt...
Lieber Gott, so denkt er, welch ein Regen!
Und er spannt den Schirm auf, den er hat.

Doch am Himmel tut sich nichts bewegen,
und kein Windhauch rührt ein Blatt.
Gleichwohl darf man jenen Argwohn hegen.

Denn das Pflaster, über das er wandelt,
ist vom Magistrat voll List – gesprenkelt.
Bona fide hat der Gast gehandelt.

11. Palmström lobt

Palmström lobt das schlechte Wetter sehr,
denn dann ist auf Erden viel mehr Ruhe;
ganz von selbst beschränkt sich das Getue,
und der Mensch geht würdiger einher.

Schon allein des Schirmes kleiner Himmel
wirkt symbolisch auf des Menschen Kern,
denn der wirkliche ist dem Gewimmel,
ach nicht ihm nur, leider noch recht fern.

Durch die Gassen oder im Gefilde
wandert Palmström, wenn die Wolke fällt,
und erfreut sich an dem Menschenbilde,
das sich kosmo-logischer verhält.

12. Muhme Kunkel

Palma Kunkel ist mit Palm verwandt,
doch im übrigen sonst nicht bekannt.
Und sie wünscht auch nicht bekannt zu sein,
lebt am liebsten ganz für sich allein.

Über Muhme Palma Kunkel drum
bleibt auch der Chronist vollkommen stumm.
Nur wo selbst sie aus dem Dunkel tritt,
teilt er dies ihr Treten treulich mit.

Doch sie trat bis jetzt noch nicht ans Licht,
und sie will es auch in Zukunft nicht.
Schon, daß hier ihr Name lautbar ward,
widerspricht vollkommen ihrer Art.

13. Im Tierkostüm

Palmström liebt es, Tiere nachzuahmen,
und erzieht zwei junge Schneider
lediglich auf Tierkostüme.

So z. B. hockt er gern als Rabe
auf dem oberen Aste einer Eiche
und beobachtet den Himmel.

Häufig auch als Bernhardiner
legt er zottigen Kopf auf tapfere Pfoten,
bellt im Schlaf und träumt gerettete Wanderer.

Oder spinnt ein Netz in seinem Garten
aus Spagat und sitzt als eine Spinne
tagelang in dessen Mitte.

Oder schwimmt, ein glotzgeäugter Karpfen,
rund um die Fontäne seines Teiches
und erlaubt den Kindern, ihn zu füttern.

Oder hängt sich im Kostüm des Storches
unter eines Luftschiffs Gondel
und verreist so nach Ägypten.

14. Das böhmische Dorf

Palmström reist, mit einem Herrn v. Korf,
in ein sogenanntes böhmisches Dorf.

Unverständlich bleibt ihm alles dort,
von dem ersten bis zum letzten Wort.

Auch v. Korf (der nur des Reimes wegen
ihn begleitet) ist um Rat verlegen.

Doch just dieses macht ihn blaß vor Glück.
Tief entzückt kehrt unser Freund zurück.

Und er schreibt in seine Wochenchronik:
Wieder ein Erlebnis, voll von Honig!

15. Die Korfsche Uhr

Korf erfindet eine Uhr,
die mit zwei Paar Zeigern kreist
und damit nach vorn nicht nur,
sondern auch nach rückwärts weist.

Zeigt sie zwei, – somit auch zehn;
zeigt sie drei, – somit auch neun;
und man braucht nur hinzusehn,
um die Zeit nicht mehr zu scheun.

Denn auf dieser Uhr von Korfen
mit dem janushaften Lauf
(dazu ward sie so entworfen):
hebt die Zeit sich selber auf.

16. Palmströms Uhr

Palmströms Uhr ist andrer Art,
reagiert mimosisch zart.

Wer sie bittet, wird empfangen.
Oft schon ist sie so gegangen,

wie man herzlich sie gebeten,
ist zurück- und vorgetreten,

eine Stunde, zwei, drei Stunden,
je nachdem sie mitempfunden.

Selbst als Uhr, mit ihren Zeiten,
will sie nicht Prinzipien reiten:

Zwar ein Werk, wie allerwärts,
doch zugleich ein Werk – mit Herz.

17. Die Mausefalle I

Palmström hat nicht Speck im Haus,
dahingegen eine Maus.

Korf, bewegt von seinem Jammer,
baut ihm eine Gitterkammer.

Und mit einer Geige fein
setzt er seinen Freund hinein.

Nacht ist's, und die Sterne funkeln.
Palmström musiziert im Dunkeln.

Und derweil er konzertiert,
kommt die Maus hereinspaziert.

Hinter ihr, geheimerweise,
fällt die Pforte leicht und leise.

Vor ihr sinkt in Schlaf alsbald
Palmströms schweigende Gestalt.

II

Morgens kommt v. Korf und lädt
das so nützliche Gerät

in den nächsten, sozusagen
mittelgroßen Möbelwagen,

den ein starkes Roß beschwingt
nach der fernen Waldung bringt,

wo in tiefer Einsamkeit
er das seltne Paar befreit.

Erst spaziert die Maus heraus
und dann Palmström, nach der Maus.

Froh genießt das Tier der neuen
Heimat, ohne sich zu scheuen.

Während Palmström, glückverklärt,
mit v. Korf nach Hause fährt.

18. Die beiden Feste

Korf und Palmström geben je ein Fest.

Dieser lädt die ganze Welt zu Gaste:
doch allein zum Zwecke, daß sie – faste!
einen Tag lang sich mit nichts belaste!
Und ein – Antihungersnotfonds ist der Rest.

Korf hingegen wandert zu den Armen,
zu den Krüppeln und den leider Schlimmen
und versucht sie alle so zu stimmen,
daß sie einen Tag lang nicht ergrimmen,
daß in ihnen anhebt aufzuglimmen
ein jedweden ›Feind‹ umfassendes – Erbarmen.

Beide lassen so die Menschen schenken
statt genießen, und sie meinen: freuen
könnten Wesen (die nun einmal – *denken*)
sich allein an solchen gänzlich neuen Festen.

19. Der eingebundene Korf

Korf läßt sich in einen Folianten einbinden,
um selben immer bei sich zu tragen;
die Rücken liegen gemeinsam hinten,
doch vorn ist das Buch auseinandergeschlagen.
So daß er, gleichsam flügelbelastet,
mit hinter den Armen flatternden Seiten
hinwandelt oder zu anderen Zeiten
in seinen Flügeln blätternd rastet.

20. Europens Bücher

Korf ist fassungslos, und er entflieht,
wenn er nur Europens Bücher sieht.

Er versteht es nicht, wie man
zentnerschwere Bände leiden kann.

Und ihm graut, wie man dadurch den Geist
gleichsam in ein Grab von Stoff verweist.

Geist ist leicht und sollte darum auch
leicht gewandet gehn nach Geisterbrauch.

Doch der Europäer ruht erst dann,
wenn er ihn in Bretter "binden" kann.

21. Der fromme Riese

Korf lernt einen Riesen kennen,
dessen Frau ihm alles in den Mund gibt,
was sie nicht mag.

Nacht und Tag,
wenn sie ihm solchen Willen kundgibt,
sieht man ihn seine Lippen geduldig trennen

und vorsichtig hinter sein Zahngehege
alles schieben, was seiner Frau im Wege.

Und es ist ihr viel im Wege, der Frau.
Ganz unmöglich wäre, zu sagen genau,

was von Mücke bis Mammut gewissermaßen
ihr mißfällt. Man findet da ganze Straßen,
ganze Städte voll Menschen, man findet Gärten,

Flüsse, Berge neben Perücken, Bärten,
Stöcken, Tellern, Kleidern; mit einem Worte:
eine Welt versammelt sich an gedachtem Orte.

v. Korf mißfällt und wird von dem frommen
Riesengatten still in den Mund genommen.

Und nur, weil er ein ›Geist‹, wie schon beschrieben,
ist er nicht in diesem Gelaß verblieben.

22. Die zwei Wurzeln

Zwei Tannenwurzeln groß und alt
unterhalten sich im Wald.

Was droben in den Wipfeln rauscht,
das wird hier unten ausgetauscht.

Ein altes Eichhorn sitzt dabei
und strickt wohl Strümpfe für die zwei.

Die eine sagt: knig. Die andre sagt: knag.
Das ist genug für einen Tag.

23. Der Leu

Auf einem Wandkalenderblatt
ein Leu sich abgebildet hat.

Er blickt dich an, bewegt und still,
den ganzen 17. April.

Wodurch er zu erinnern liebt,
daß es ihn immerhin noch gibt.

24. Windegesprach

"Hast nie die Welt gesehn?
Hammerfest - Wien - Athen?"

"Nein, ich kenne nur dies Tal,
bin nur so ein Lokalwind –

kennst du Kuntzens Tanzsaal?"

"Nein, Kind.
Servus! Muß davon!
Köln - Paris - Lissabon."

25. Die beiden Esel

Ein finstrer Esel sprach einmal
zu seinem ehlichen Gemahl:

“Ich bin so dumm, du bist so dumm,
wir wollen sterben gehen, kumm!”

Doch wie es kommt so öfter eben:
Die beiden blieben fröhlich leben.

26. Der Lattenzaun

Es war einmal ein Lattenzaun,
mit Zwischenraum, hindurchzuschaun.

Ein Architekt, der dieses sah,
stand eines Abends plötzlich da –

und nahm den Zwischenraum heraus
und baute draus ein großes Haus.

Der Zaun indessen stand ganz dumm,
mit Latten ohne was herum.

Ein Anblick gräßlich und gemein.
Drum zog ihn der Senat auch ein.

Der Architekt jedoch entfloh
nach Afri-od- Ameriko.

27. Der Schnupfen

Ein Schnupfen hockt auf der Terrasse,
auf daß er sich ein Opfer fasse

– und stürzt alsbald mit großem Grimm
auf einen Menschen namens Schrimm.

Paul Schrimm erwidert prompt: »Pitschü!«
und *hat* ihn drauf bis Montag früh.

28. Denkmalswunsch

Setze mir ein Denkmal, cher,
ganz aus Zucker, tief im Meer.

Ein Süßwassersee, zwar kurz,
werd ich dann nach meinem Sturz;

doch so lang, daß Fische, hundert,
nehmen einen Schluck verwundert. –

Diese ißt in Hamburg und
Bremen dann des Menschen Mund. –

Wiederum in eure Kreise
komm ich so auf gute Weise,

während, werd ich Stein und Erz,
nur ein Vogel seinen Sterz

oder gar ein Mensch von Wert
seinen Witz auf mich entleert.

29. Das Huhn

In der Bahnhofhalle, nicht für es gebaut,
geht ein Huhn
hin und her ...
Wo, wo ist der Herr Stationsvorsteh'r?
Wird dem Huhn
man nichts tun?
Hoffen wir es! Sagen wir es laut:
daß ihm unsre Sympathie gehört,
selbst an dieser Stätte, wo es – "stört!"

30. Das Knie

Ein Knie geht einsam durch die Welt.
Es ist ein Knie, sonst nichts!
Es ist kein Baum! Es ist kein Zelt!
Es ist ein Knie, sonst nichts.

Im Kriege ward einmal ein Mann
erschossen um und um.
Das Knie allein blieb unverletzt –
als wärs ein Heiligtum.

Seitdem gehts einsam durch die Welt.
Es ist ein Knie, sonst nichts.
Es ist kein Baum, es ist kein Zelt.
Es ist ein Knie, sonst nichts.

CPSIA information can be obtained
at www.ICGtesting.com
Printed in the USA
BVHW091716160221
600245BV00015B/459

9 780986 066207